It is no mystery that you hold this book in your hand, for there are no mysteries in life, only understanding. Individuals at various times during their cosmic journey find themselves either in the cosmic flow, fighting against its current, or waiting on the shore looking for the opportune moment to jump in. The time is now, and in your hands there is a cosmic clue;
find your flow and jump in.

Intention

It is my greatest hope that the words, thoughts, and resolutions within the following pages will help each of us to be a better person, husband, wife, friend, and cosmic citizen. If you find but one resolution that resonates within the garden of your soul, we will be kindred spirits and our world will be better as a result.

Inspiration

It is a small wonder that the citizens of the world commit themselves to setting resolutions only once a year, instead of living a life built around the foundation resolutions provide. They set a resolution for losing weight or saving money, instead of creating a lifestyle built around healthy eating and proper budgeting. Imagine the harvest a farmer could expect if she/he planted but one seed a year. How bountiful of a harvest could she/he expect?

Our mind is literally the metaphorical "Garden of Eden", and our "Free Will" its master gardener. The conscious gardener knows that resolutions are to the mind what the plow is to the land, they are tools for the initial cultivation of the mind, for the sowing of good thought-seeds. These thought-seeds, whether planted purposefully or accidentally, manifest themselves in our complete character and the circumstances we experience.

The consistent repetition or sowing of good resolutions turns over the upper layers of our limiting beliefs, while burying negative thoughts and irrational assumptions. It is thus that we empower our mind with fresh ideas which rekindle that cosmic spark within us.

We become in time what we commit to the soil of our mind, and there is no exception to this cosmic law of sowing and reaping. The ancients who said, "Know Thyself", knew what they were planting, and their ancient gardens to this day reflect it. The pyramids in Giza are still revealing the resolutions they must have planted in the gardens of their mind.

Resolve to know that resolutions help us to consciously create the self we imagine; and good resolutions become in time our greatest assets and our fondest teachers. Within our vast imaginative mind is literally our Garden of Eden; let us plant something magical, create something majestic.

I am, you are, we are resolved to evolve; we know we become that which we emit through time.

Dictionary

Resolve v. (resolved, resolving)
1. To make up one's mind; to decide firmly.

2. To solve, explain, or settle.

3. A firm mental decision or intention; determination.

Example:
> Resolve to be a Possibility Advocate for your family, friends, strangers, and yourself.

Kemit Affirmationary
"We become what we emit through time."

Resolve v. (resolved, resolving)

1. I made up my mind; you can make up your mind; we can make up our mind; we can come to a decision about a plan of action. **We are resolved.**

2. You can decide firmly; I can decide firmly; we can decide firmly; resistant to externally applied pressure, fixed; we can come to a resolution in our mind as the direct result of our deliberation. **We are resolved.**

3. I can solve my challenges; you can solve your challenges; we have the ability to solve our challenges; we can find an answer, work out the solution to the challenges before us. **We are resolved.**

4. We can make a firm mental decision; I can make a firm mental decision; you can make a firm mental decision; in our resolute and determined manner, our decisions are solid, unyielding to emotion, impenetrable to doubt. **We are resolved.**

5. I have firmness of purpose; you have firmness of purpose; we have firmness of purpose; we are resilient to obstacles and impediments; we are impervious to skepticism, indecision or hesitation in any form. **We are resolved.**

Dictionary

Evolve v. (evolved, evolving)
1. to emit

2. to develop gradually from simple to complex form

3. to come forth gradually into being

4. to change slowly

5. to undergo evolutionary change

6. to achieve gradually

Example:

Resolve to evolve.

Kemit Affirmationary

"We become what we emit through time."

Evolve v. (evolved, evolving)

1. You emit; I emit, we emit; we send out, we transmit positive intentions, bold resolve, courageous and committed thoughts and ideals, from one place or person to another. We radiate our highest self always. We **evolve.**

2. I develop gradually; you develop gradually; we develop gradually, growing in small degrees, steadily advancing from a simple to a more complex and capable being. We **evolve.**

3. You change slowly; I change slowly; we undergo transition consciously, passing from one phase to another, transmuting and transforming ourselves, we effectively become different, we change through time. We **evolve.**

4. We, you and I, are constantly and consciously undergoing evolutionary change, we are engaged in a process of growth from our lower, simpler selves, to our higher, more disciplined, committed and self-reliant nature. We **evolve.**

5. I achieve gradually; you achieve gradually; we achieve gradually; we carry out our designs step-by-step, little-by-little, accomplishing our aim through consistent, unwavering effort and exertion; we attain our desired end gradually through time. We **evolve.**

Resolve to evolve.
I am resolved to evolve;
You are resolved to evolve;
We are resolved to evolve.

We change the words we use to
define ourselves, the thoughts we
entertain about who we are and
what we are capable of. We change
our habits and our character
gradually, slowly, one resolution at a
time.
We are committed to
Sowing and planting,
One resolution at a time
Into our heart and mind,
And into the hearts and minds of
Humanity.
We, you and I are,
Resolved to evolve.

0 **Resolve to evolve.**

1 Resolve to be known as one with an unmatchable drive and commitment to succeed.

2 Resolve to be willing to fail to achieve your goals.

3 Resolve to accept the fact that you may fall short of reaching your ideal, but always put forth your best effort.

4 Resolve to begin all endeavors with wild expectations of success.

5 Resolve to never make excuses for your shortcomings or failures.

6 Resolve to create within your mind an environment conducive and receptive to the attainment of your aim and your purpose.

7   Resolve to dream, plan, act, and repeat this process again and again until you bring to fruition that which you desire to achieve.

8   Resolve to challenge your fears, your doubts, and your weaknesses.

9   Resolve to step up your game whenever you meet with disappointment or defeat.

10 Resolve to respect failure and to harness it to your advantage.

11 Resolve to fix your sight upon your aim, set your heart upon doing it, and let nothing interfere with your progress.

12 Resolve to avoid the people or things which tend to stimulate and stir up impure passions or negative emotions.

13 Resolve to express yourself without using profanity; disappointment needs no further encouragement.

14 Resolve to seek the highest wisdom in every situation.

15 Resolve not to shrink from the hard task of beginning.

16 Resolve to constantly seek and strive for improvement in all your undertakings.

17 Resolve to cease from dissipating your energies and instead, focus your attention and efforts towards building something worthwhile.

18 Resolve to understand that truth and success are ultimately one because we cannot trust the wrong means to reach the right goal.

19   Resolve to identify, uproot, and conquer your vices.

20   Resolve to think only about what will be beneficial to you and others.

21   Resolve to continually evoke thoughts and images of the person you desire to become, of the ideal you have imagined.

22   Resolve to seek and identify opportunities.

23   Resolve never to complain of a lost chance; act now as if your life depended upon it.

24   Resolve to look for the good in everyone, in everything, in every situation.

25   Resolve to make your will and your intellect act in unison.

26   Resolve to concentrate your thoughts and energy upon the ideas you are working on; focus your attention, harness the power of your will.

27   Resolve to help others when you can.

28   Resolve not to imitate or copy the poor habits of others or your previous self. Do not transgress.

29   Resolve to overcome your undesirable impulses and behaviors.

30   Resolve to think problems and challenges through to the end.

31   Resolve to be loyal and faithful to family, friends, yourself, and your ideals.

32 Resolve to make time for the things you want to achieve.

33 Resolve to contemplate your opinions and to speak to facts. Do not mistake opinions for facts.

34 Resolve to impress upon your mind and body a spirit of cheerfulness and endurance.

35 Resolve to be faithful and obedient to your intuition as it urges you to do and to be your best at the moment when you feel like giving up; fight back.

36 Resolve to be a good worker, competent and assured in all that you undertake.

Inspiration

We, you and I, have the power to decide, to make a choice. We are able to come to a resolution, to find an answer, a solution to the challenges we face, the opportunities we have yet to seize before us.

We, you and I, can make up our own mind; we can make our own commitments; we have been making choices, deciding, and determining the course of our thoughts and actions our whole lives.

Kemit Affirmationary
"We become what we emit through time."

37   Resolve to be calm as water in adversity, just in all your dealings; stay centered, find balance.

38   Resolve to get along with people.

39   Resolve to defeat the angel of despair with action, vigorous and sustained.

40   Resolve to confront challenges rather than dodge them.

41   Resolve to abandon perfectionism; it suffocates initiative and promotes fear.

42   Resolve to cultivate your personal magnetism through honesty, energy, and poise.

43 Resolve to habitually practice, in all your social interactions, small acts of kindness, courtesies, and considerations.

44 Resolve to persevere in detaching yourself from your emotional and sensual conditioning.

45 Resolve to identify and find unity with your indwelling intelligence for it regulates your breathing, blood flow, heartbeat, and healing; it guides all things.

46 Resolve to transcend your identification with your limiting beliefs.

47 Resolve to work your ideas up in your mind and heart until they catch fire and compel you to act.

48   Resolve to develop your capacity to sustain deep and protracted thought.

49   Resolve to uncover the truth in every situation, rather than pursue information, which simply supports your beliefs.

50   Resolve to abandon preconceived notions of things and events.

51   Resolve to follow the truth, wherever it leads you.

52   Resolve to detach yourself from undesirable people, places, and behaviors.

53   Resolve to raise your energy level to match the tasks you face.

54   Resolve to know and understand that truth is neither beautiful nor ugly, it just is, do not take it personal.

55   Resolve to know the difference between how you wish things to be, how things appear to be, and how they actually are.

56   Resolve to be truthful and trustworthy to yourself and to others.

57   Resolve to know and understand that nature pardons no mistake, but you can. Have the courage to forgive.

58   Resolve not to be deceived by the appearance of things; learn to trust, but verify.

Perfectionism

Is a belief that a state of completeness and flawlessness can and should be attained. It is a belief that work or output that is anything less than perfect is unacceptable.

Tens of millions of ideas are never pursued because the originators of those ideas were plagued by perfectionism and doubt. The resolution below gave me the courage to publish "Resolved to Evolve" unedited. Our ideas are worthy, have the courage to pursue them.

Resolution 41

Resolve to abandon perfectionism; it Suffocates initiative and promotes fear.

59 Resolve to pursue truth to understand reality.

60 Resolve to see the world as it is.

61 Resolve not to fight against time, embrace delays.

62 Resolve to improve the effectiveness of your thinking by assimilating methods which enable you to arrive at the truth quickly.

63 Resolve to acknowledge things as they are, but know that not all things need to be accepted as they are; change.

64 Resolve to strive in spite of difficulties; bamboo may bend in the wind, but seldom does it break.

65 Resolve to find pleasure in the effort of pursuing a demanding goal.

66 Resolve to do, to strive, to build, to live.

67 Resolve to identify the small wonders in your work that bring you joy.

68 Resolve to fortify your soul by doing meaningful work.

69 Resolve to be the person that is synonymous with action; cultivate decisiveness, be the verb.

70 Resolve to contribute to and encourage the prosperity of others.

71 Resolve to seek happiness in the overcoming of difficulties.

72 Resolve to enjoy your learning, growing, and accomplishing.

73 Resolve to work towards happiness by pursuing challenging and worthy goals.

74 Resolve to grow spiritually, mentally and financially.

75 Resolve to conquer circumstances, solve problems, and achieve goals.

76 Resolve to dwell in environments that will best develop, mold, and shape you towards the ideal you imagine.

77 Resolve to never abandon or waste your talents.

78 Resolve to stay away from people and places that belittle your ambitions.

79　Resolve to create favorable conditions for the implementation of your plans.

80　Resolve to surround yourself with characters you wish to emulate, and fill your mind with stories of the great people you admire.

81　Resolve to strengthen your power to accomplish by developing your will power. Believe that you can and you will.

82　Resolve to develop your achievement muscle through exercise; overcome doubt with action, fear with courage.

83　Resolve to find work which is a perpetual tonic to you, which broadens and deepens your experience, and forces you to grow.

84 Resolve to do what nature intended for you to do; do what you are good at.

85 Resolve to find a way to make a living by doing the work that you think about the most.

86 Resolve to be encouraged, not discouraged, with every wrong attempt.

87 Resolve to overcome the negative by not identifying with it; learn to let go.

88 Resolve to pay the price of achievement in effort and time.

89 Resolve to think with passion and purpose.

Inspiration

"Many times we know intellectually that we should do this or that thing, but we avoid doing it because we lack the "Will" to take action. Sometimes we cannot put our fingers on the why, other times it is a reality we would rather avoid."

Resolution 25

Resolve to make your "Will" and your intellect act in unison.

Inspiration

Our resolutions are our pledge,
our pledge our word.
Committed, we are bound by
our resolutions as the tree is
bound to the earth, as water is
bound to the sea, as breath is
bound to life, and as our life is
bound to do the work of Good.

Kemit Affirmationary
"We become what we emit through time."

90   Resolve to make the unconditional commitment to complete your objectives and reach your goals.

91   Resolve to intensify the strength of your decisions through your unwavering devotion to their successful implementation.

92   Resolve to view defeats and setbacks as installments for future victories.

93   Resolve to intensify your concentration upon the intended desired effect until it manifests.

94   Resolve to pursue with passion and conviction your desired aim, and to make up your mind to win in spite of all repulses and defeats.

95   Resolve to leave no mistake without the accompanying wisdom.

Inspiration

There once lived a cantankerous old man who dreamt he had died and gone to heaven. It was early in the morning and the sun had just begun to crest over the horizon; it was a new day.

Startled the old man looked around for the familiar signs of heaven. Where were the big fluffy white clouds, the angels playing harps, the children walking, laughing, and singing? This is strange he thought to himself. I know I am in heaven, so where is everyone, and where are the things I thought would be here?

A short time passed before the old man realized that though he was in heaven, he was still on earth. A peace came over him as happiness filled his heart, a joy too wonderful to explain. He realized at that moment heaven was on earth, only now he was looking at everything differently. In heaven he viewed everyone through the lens of possibility rather than of his old lens of doubt, fear, and despair.

As the old man descended the mountain and headed towards his home, he could hardly wait to love those who had showed him love. He looked forward to smiling at the others for no other reason than just being alive. Most of all, he looked forward to having fun with the children he used to scold. He could hardly wait to walk and laugh, laugh and walk, smile and sing while doing all the things he could imagine.

Resolution 135
Resolve to acknowledge the
small miracles in your daily life.

96   Resolve to educate yourself through defeat, loss, setback, failure, and every repulse.

97   Resolve to make an ally of failure, master it to know victory.

98   Resolve to befriend success and abandon your fear of failure.

99   Resolve to make as many mistakes as are necessary to reach the desired outcome.

100   Resolve not to allow your lack of understanding to stop you from trying.

101   Resolve to respect the fact that people have their own ideas and opinions.

102   Resolve to laugh when you find yourself frustrated by trivial matters.

103   Resolve never to consent to feelings of inferiority.

104   Resolve to accept that everything happens for a reason; therefore, seek to understand the cause, and the effect will be clear.

105   Resolve to always make the best of the way things turn out.

106   Resolve to make the law of averages serve your purpose by trying harder and more often to succeed.

107   Resolve to take more risks to improve your odds of success.

108   Resolve to be curious.

109   Resolve that your attitude will
            not be dispirited by exterior
            negative feelings and happenings.

110   Resolve to respond to events, not
            to react to them; most times no
            response is the best response.

111   Resolve to express sympathy for
            Others who try to hurt your
            Feelings with their thoughts,
            Opinions, and actions for they
            Reveal their own suffering.

112   Resolve to understand that no
            one can hurt you unless you
            accept the hurt in your mind and
            heart.

113   Resolve to know that not all soil is
            conducive for planting, and all
            thoughts and ideas need not be
            shared.

114   Resolve to know that a positive response to your ideas by family and friends is not a requirement for the success or viability of your ideas.

115   Resolve to value your time by making lists and setting priorities.

116   Resolve to review your priorities constantly and to always ask: what is the best use of my time right now?

117   Resolve to consistently ask the questions: what is the payoff in doing this activity, how does it fit into my short, mid, and long-term plans?

118   Resolve to make decisions and act upon them.

Inspiration

Will, my will, your will, our will is a birthright, an honor and privilege to cherish, cultivate, master and behold. Possessing the ability to decide is a freedom we should defend. Unwavering and unwilling to relinquish, a right we are indebted to uphold, one we are compelled never to abandon, "Will Power", is ours to defend. Rise from your seat, stand with your feet firmly on the ground, transcend want to be one with your word, an extension of our spirit, the living word, our living commitment to be.

We, you and I, are **volition. We are "Will", incarnate in flesh for the Good of humanity,** and no one can take this away from us. Moved by spirit, invigorate your "Will" through an unwavering commitment to be.

Kemit Affirmationary

"We become what we emit through time."

119   Resolve to have the attitude that influences circumstances, not one which is determined by them.

120   Resolve to plan your work and work your plan, and always seek ways to improve your efforts.

121   Resolve to give meaning to time by using it wisely and with foresight.

122   Resolve to prioritize your tasks and to do first all the things which ought to be done, before doing the things which you would like to do.

123   Resolve to concentrate your mind, thoughts, and energy upon the essentials for the greatest possible results.

124 Resolve to fear no man or thing. Know that the universe is infinite and cannot be destroyed. Acknowledge that you are a constituent of infinity, therefore you cannot be destroyed.

125 Resolve never to allow doubt to stop you from attempting to do something meaningful or significant.

126 Resolve to undertake mighty tasks, even though some setbacks may occur; commit to finish all that you undertake.

127 Resolve never to allow fear of disappointment or embarrassment to deter you from doing a thing you feel compelled to do.

128   Resolve to master your management of time through better management of your activities within it.

129   Resolve to immunize yourself from fear by constantly exposing yourself to the things you fear.

130   Resolve to boldly walk through all obstacles, never cower before them.

131   Resolve to fight hesitancy with swift and forceful action.

132   Resolve to value all life, and know all life has purpose.

133   Resolve to build strength, courage, and confidence by doing the things you think you cannot do.

Dictionary

Mistake n. (v. mistook, mistaken, mistaking)

1. An error in action, calculation, opinion, or judgment caused by poor reasoning, carelessness, insufficient knowledge, etc.

2. Misunderstanding or misconception.

Example:
What is it about our homes and schools, and the way we teach our children which causes them to fear of making mistakes? They fear being punished, teased, ridiculed, and embarrassed before their parents and peers; this it traumatic.

Kemit Affirmationary

"We become what we emit through time."

Mistake n. (v. mistook, mistaken, mistaking)

1. You and I, we, are allowed, permitted, *to make errors in our actions, opinions, calculations and judgements* while we seek to master a subject or skill; as we strive toward our aim. **Love your mistakes, they instruct. Be curious.**

2. On occasion, you and I, we, *will err because of poor reasoning, carelessness, or because of insufficient knowledge;* this is acceptable when putting forth effort to pursue a goal. Keep pursuing, commit to improve. **Love your mistakes, they reveal our progress. Be curious.**

3. We, you and I are going to *miscalculate, blunder, fumble, fall short of our ideals*; this is normal and encouraged; refocus your attention, concentrate. **Love your mistakes, they help us to grow. Be curious.**

4. On the path towards achieving our purpose, we, you and I, will experience many joyful *gaffes, and faux pas*, this is the way of growth and fulfillment. Enjoy the moment, and then seek to understand the error. **Love your mistakes, they provide useful hints for our journey. Be curious.**

134 Resolve to believe that every breath you take is a gift from a source unseen, and know that the same invisible force wants to see you and others succeed.

135 Resolve to acknowledge the small miracles in your daily life.

136 Resolve to acknowledge the infinite intelligence which surrounds all things; it is there to help you.

137 Resolve to open your mind and eyes to the majesty of creation.

138 Resolve to advance steadily, deliberately, and without haste.

139 Resolve to develop the now habit for tomorrow is guaranteed to no one.

140   Resolve to give thanks for the blessings you expect to receive each day.

141   Resolve to have faith in good, and trust that you are worthy to receive it.

142   Resolve not to allow others to make their priority your priority.

143   Resolve to seek tirelessly for the knowledge of your true identity.

144   Resolve to exercise your power to choose.

145   Resolve to base your beliefs upon solid evidence; check the source.

146   Resolve to suspend judgment when you lack sufficient knowledge and evidence.

147　Resolve to identify sufficient reasons upon which to base your faith.

148　Resolve to rule your passions, desires, and emotions.

149　Resolve to control your thoughts by actively sowing your intentions and your will in every situation.

150　Resolve to be ruled by a clear mind and a clean heart.

151　Resolve to trust without reservation the belief that there is a way to realize your vision, live your ideal, and reach your goal.

152　Resolve to conquer the division within yourself, and move indefatigably towards inward mastery of self.

153   Resolve to take full possession of your mind. Become the rightful ruler of your internal empire, the rightful king of your dominion, the "I am I", master of the land of self.

154   Resolve to free yourself from the slavery of perception, never judge.

155   Resolve to break the hypnotic and damaging hold of your internal and external critics.

156   Resolve to break the chains of the habits which enslave you, which cause disunity between your mind, heart, and will.

157   Resolve to control your emotions when distressed; do not overreact, it will pass.

158   Resolve to be master of your own becoming. Hold steadfast to your evolution and be not deterred from this course of action.

159   Resolve to observe, understand, know, and control your internal, subjective, and sub-verbal experiences.

160   Resolve to bring clarity and light to your negative emotions and thinking. Ferret out what is true and what is false to discern what the realities are.

161   Resolve to recognize and write down your critical thoughts as they cross your mind; expose their source and their intentions. If they are valid, address them, if they are not, discard them.

162   Resolve to seek and uncover the force behind your nature, understand it and convene with it.

163   Resolve to understand the internal laws of your becoming, and then apply them to your conscious evolution.

164   Resolve not to be deceived by the illusions of your emotions, or the emotions of others.

165   Resolve to build strong habits through sound reasoning.

166   Resolve to seize every opportunity to do something rather than nothing.

Dictionary

Do v. (did, done, doing, does)
1. to perform

2. to act

3. to fulfill

4. to complete

Example:
What can I do for you?

Kemit Affirmationary

"We become what we emit through time."

Do v. (did, done, doing, does)

1. I perform, you perform, we perform; we carry out our designs and plans step-by-step. We accomplish our task, the piece of work assigned to us, efficiently and on time regardless of difficulty. **We are women and men of action, we are not talkers, we are doers; we do.**

2. I take action; you take action, we take action; we are doers of deeds, achievers par excellence, perpetually working mentally and physically to accomplish our aim. Through our own efforts, labor, we exert ourselves indefatigably; we act. **We are people of action; we are not talkers, we are doers, we do.**

3. You fulfill, I fulfill, we fulfill our promises, and we do what we commit to do. We bring to completion all that we undertake. Satisfying all requirements and obligations, we bring to a successful end everything we start. We are doers of deeds both great and small. **We aren't talkers, we are doers, women and men of action; we do.**

4. We complete what we begin, I complete what I begin, and you complete what you begin. We finish what we start, bringing together all the necessary parts we make our desires, our goals whole. **We are synonymous with action, we aren't talkers, we are doers, we strive, we toil, we work, we do.**

Inspiration

"In the beginning there is your word, and your word is your commitment; everything you make will be made by them, and without them nothing will be made."

Kemit Affirmationary

"We become what we emit through time."

Procrastination

It refers to the act of replacing high-priority actions with tasks of low priority, and thus putting off important tasks to a later time. The next time you are tempted to procrastinate, pay attention to how it makes you feel. Notice your breathing, pay close attention to how your whole body feels. Procrastinate often enough and you will feel it growing inside you. Fight the urge to procrastinate like you would fight the tide that tries to drown you. There is never a good reason to feel badly because you procrastinated.

167   Resolve to be aware of your thinking and feeling. Make what is unconscious and automatic, conscious and actionable.

168   Resolve to seek unity between what is conscious and subconscious in the operation of your mind.

169   Resolve to be driven by passion but ruled by reason.

170   Resolve to bridge the gap between your intellect and your intuition.

171   Resolve to focus your thoughts and energy upon what you can do to control your life, the circumstances right now.

172 Resolve to seek your center and to establish a friendship with your true self.

173 Resolve to solve the conflict within yourself, between who you are and who you are capable of becoming.

174 Resolve to build consensus. Tolerate no extreme; compromise and settle upon the middle.

175 Resolve to lead a life guided by reasonableness. No one likes a dictator.

176 Resolve to deny those who try to manipulate you into doing things that you are not inclined to do.

177   Resolve to remind yourself often that procrastination is a poor employer.

178   Resolve to make the flesh as willing as the spirit. The spirit knows no limit.

179   Resolve to persevere in matters of importance.

180   Resolve to respect people as they are.

181   Resolve to see people as adequate, able, and full of possibility.

182   Resolve to give more praise.

183   Resolve to plant gardens of optimism and hope into the hearts and minds of everyone you meet.

184   Resolve to prepare yourself to the point of confidence, when you know you can do what you have to do.

185   Resolve to liberate yourself from worry by determining to find a solution.

186   Resolve to learn to focus, to concentrate your attention upon the possibilities in life.

187   Resolve to raise the level of your imagination and your thinking to the level of the possibilities before you.

188   Resolve to try again and again until you discover the keys to your success; persistence is a skill.

189   Resolve to pay positive attention to the people in your life.

190   Resolve to perceive the potentials and strengths of individuals and things instead of their weaknesses.

191   Resolve to develop your ability to match your potential; demand more of yourself.

192   Resolve to seek the cumulative effect of your efforts; trees do not grow overnight.

193   Resolve to neutralize strong inner urges that tempt you to do the things you ought not to do.

194   Resolve to invoke the life force dormant inside you to transform yourself; you are the maker and the made, the creator and the creation.

195   Resolve to believe in the words you sow into the garden of self; once planted, act vigorously to implement them; from them will spring both your plans and actions.

196   Resolve to plan and track your progress; know where you are going to, and have some idea when you will get there.

197   Resolve to practice the habits and routines you wish to form; practice them steadily.

198   Resolve to act upon the possibilities which life affords you.

199   Resolve to be prepared for the opportunities which will come your way.

Inspiration

Feeling discouraged about her size, an Acorn looked up at the big Oak next to her and asked, "What can I do to be as tall as you someday?" The big Oak looked upon his smaller neighbor and replied in a confident voice, "Commit to increase your productivity by .05% each day, and commit to reduce the number of your daily distractions by the same. That was the advice given to me a hundred years ago by the Great Oak next to me." The young acorn took his advice and is now one of the tallest trees in the forest.

200   Resolve to visualize your final destination and to seek tirelessly to find the best routes to get you there.

201   Resolve to find a plan, a roadmap of someone who has accomplished what you desire; read it, study it, then write and follow your own.

202   Resolve to do one thing every day that you know needs to be done but you have avoided doing. Delay and procrastination are related, they impede progress.

203   Resolve to pursue workable methods for the achievement of your aim.

204 Resolve to be meticulous in your planning, miss not one detail when creating the system for the eventual attainment of your goals and objectives.

205 Resolve to create a definite step-by-step plan to carry you through to your goal, and then follow that plan to completion.

206 Resolve to stay on the straight road, avoid at all cost side roads and shortcuts.

207 Resolve to have constantly in mind, and before your eyes, the state of your affairs; and harbor no illusions about the time you have to affect them.

208 Resolve to master the tools of planning, time and energy management; know your energy cycle.

209 Resolve to keep at the forefront of your mind what you are going to do to get what you want.

210 Resolve to determine what it is that you want from this life, your life.

211 Resolve to seek the path or cut a path from where you are to where you want to be.

212 Resolve not to rely upon chance or providence to provide what you seek; rely upon your planning, your action, and your faith.

213   Resolve to have hope in your dreams, and give hope to others who dare to dream.

214   Resolve to encourage within yourself and others a discerning eye for detail.

215   Resolve to try harder after each setback, adjust, re-commit yourself and push forward renewed.

216   Resolve to acknowledge your oneness with the all-pervading wisdom and power of the universe.

217   Resolve to avoid using mind-altering substances to escape from undesired realities.

218   Resolve to think often about the end-result of your endeavors, the feelings of elation, of satisfaction, and joy.

219   Resolve to believe and have confidence that you can win if you remain committed.

220   Resolve to believe something good will happen in the moment you need it most.

221   Resolve to expect the best results in every situation and all your endeavors.

222   Resolve to improve your outlook; in your mind, shape events to meet your expectations.

223   Resolve to have a receptive attitude towards the possibility of achievement.

224   Resolve to expect much, to expect grand things from honest, consistent effort to realize your dreams.

225   Resolve to have complete trust in your ability. Inside the Acorn a one-hundred-foot Oak Tree sleeps. You can do it.

226   Resolve to question the thoughts and feelings which cause anxiety.

227   Resolve to commit to your aspirations, and continue to seek evidence and resources to support them.

228   Resolve that things will go your way.

229   Resolve that under challenging and unpredictable circumstances the highest good will be done.

Commitment

"Until one is committed, there is hesitancy, the chance to draw back, always ineffectiveness. Concerning all acts of initiative (and creation), there is one elementary truth the ignorance of which kills countless ideas and splendid plans: that the moment one definitely commits oneself, then providence moves too. A whole stream of events issues from the decision, raising in one's favor all manner of unforeseen incidents, meetings and material assistance, which no man could have dreamt would have come his way. I learned a deep respect for one of Goethe's couplets:

'Whatever you can do or dream you can, begin it. Boldness has genius, power and magic in it!'"

(*W. H. Murry*)

230 Resolve to master future events and potential situations with forethought and preparation.

231 Resolve to maintain a sound mind in order to make responsible decisions.

232 Resolve to be consistent.

233 Resolve to do more than what you are paid for.

234 Resolve to renew yourself every day; acknowledge that the next moment is new, the day is new, and if you can still take a breath, you still have a chance to make things better.

235 Resolve at the onset of any endeavor to remain steadfast, unwavering, committed.

236   Resolve to eliminate errors and inefficiencies from your thinking, planning, and doing.

237   Resolve to be resourceful. When possible, think ahead, consider every alternative.

238   Resolve to recognize obstacles, unfavorable circumstances, and impediments as the necessary fuel to fire your ambitions.

239   Resolve at the beginning of each day to do more than you did the day before. Improve upon your efforts in the smallest degree knowing their accumulated effect will bring the greatest return.

240   Resolve to understand the requirements of your task or assignment, then find ways to go beyond what is required.

241   Resolve to maintain the highest standards for yourself; do not settle for less.

242   Resolve to never be content with mediocrity; it is like a rash that grows, and it will eventually cover every part of your life.

243   Resolve to focus and pursue the wealth of your ideas, not the money you think they will bring.

244   Resolve to uncover the fount of all wealth and achievement: clear thought.

245   Resolve to overcome the perils of inertia by having the courage to act, the willingness to begin.

246   Resolve to go beyond the call of duty, to do more than others expect by striving for excellence in all you undertake.

247   Resolve to have a goal at every stage of life.

248   Resolve to seek the benefits of a fully functioning, well-tuned mind. Read, do lots of math, and find ways to increase the blood and oxygen flow to your brain.

249   Resolve to bring to fruition the ideas which come from being inspired; tap into the conscious flow of creation.

250   Resolve to create and work from a checklist.

251 Resolve never to allow lack of money or support to stop you from pursuing a worthwhile goal or idea.

252 Resolve to have something to be thankful for every night you go to sleep.

253 Resolve to make life worth living by finding something worth working for.

254 Resolve to do something different every week; discover, explore, learn something new, surprise someone.

255 Resolve to avoid communicating your point of view when angry or frustrated.

256 Resolve to acknowledge improvements and achievements.

257   Resolve to seek ways to help others; volunteer, give to charity.

258   Resolve to continually set, and pursue to completion, goals that give meaning to your life.

259   Resolve that after you achieve one goal or objective, you will immediately set another.

260   Resolve to have a purpose in life, a purpose in thought, and a purpose in action.

261   Resolve to say thank you. Always express gratitude to others when they say or do something for you.

262   Resolve to sow seeds of hope, possibility, and energy into every person, event, and situation, everything you look upon.

Dictionary

Planner n.

1. a person who plans

2. a book or desk calendar, for recording appointments, things to be done

3. a list or chart with information that is an aid to planning

Example:
Can we hire a planner to assist?

Kemit Affirmationary

"We become what we emit through time"

Planner n.

1. I am a planner, you are a planner, we are planners; we make plans for the hour, day, month, year and decade. We plan our lives. We plan and execute our designs; that is what we do, that is who we are. We are planners.

2. We, you and I, we decide which goals and objectives are to be focused upon this hour, this day, tomorrow, next week, next month and next year. With total concentration we determine how our objectives will be achieved. We are planners, we make plans and see them through to completion. We are planners; that is what we do.

3. You and I, we, keep a written account of the intended future course of action we will take towards our objectives. We manage and monitor resources and time lines for daily task achievement. We know where we stand and what needs to be done next. We are planners; that is what you and I do.

4. We, you and I, manage the details concerning what needs to be done, when it gets done, how it gets done, and by whom it will be done. Taking into account best case, expected case, and worst case scenarios you and I plan. We are planners, we make plans, allocate resources and we execute; that's what we do.

5. We are planners, you and I, we formulate strategies to achieve our ambitions. We arrange or if necessary, we will create the means required to bring to fruition our designs. We implement, direct, and monitor all steps in their proper sequence. We develop task list and the schedules required. Once the Plan has been created we get to work. Planning is what we do, it is in our DNA, and planners are who we are. Planning is what you and I do.

263   Resolve to attach your thoughts, actions, and your will to the tireless pursuit of a significant definite aim.

264   Resolve to sow the seeds for the harvest you hope to reap: spiritually, mentally, emotionally, physically, professionally and financially.

265   Resolve not to worry about things you cannot control. Worry about money repels it. Worry about health makes one sick.

266   Resolve to be content, to be happy; radiate an atmosphere of good fellowship, convey an attitude which projects to others a state favored by luck and fortune.

267   Resolve that you will not interrupt anyone when they are talking and cease to talk when others interrupt.

268   Resolve to appreciate the things you have and those with whom you enjoy them.

269   Resolve to listen intently to others and learn to compromise.

270   Resolve not to grieve for the things which you do not have, but rather rejoice for those which you have: life, family, purpose.

271   Resolve not to seek work for the riches it will bring, but rather the fulfillment it gives. Find the work that resonates with you.

272   Resolve never to scold anyone for something they did in the past, rather encourage them to seek the wisdom concealed in the experience.

273   Resolve to stay or move away from people, places, and that tolerate aggressive attitudes.

274   Resolve to keep all your commitments, fulfill every promise.

275   Resolve never to intentionally hurt anyone's feelings.

276   Resolve to eliminate the contradictions within.

277   Resolve to know it is not your job to point out the faults of others, nor must you participate when others are doing so.

278 Resolve to refrain from aggression and intimidation towards others.

279 Resolve to only give advice when asked.

280 Resolve to remember people's names, write them down, and remember something about them.

281 Resolve to be excellent in at least one area of your life.

282 Resolve to be frugal and save.

283 Resolve not to gossip or speak ill of others.

284 Resolve to be organized.

285 Resolve to find ways to provide products and services which others will pay for, and hold fast to the ideas which resonate most within you.

286 Resolve not to share bad news at night, it can wait until morning.

287 Resolve to avoid going to bed angry.

288 Resolve never to offend the honor of anyone. Insults to one's honor may be forgiven but not forgotten.

289 Resolve that you will not betray the confidence of those who trust you. If someone shares something with you in confidence, keep it confidential.

290   Resolve to always leave things and places in a better state.

291   Resolve not to comment upon the appearance of others.

292   Resolve to let those around you know when you are out of sorts.

293   Resolve to arrive at your destination early, at the very least on time.

294   Resolve to keep orderly financial records, secure your assets, and plan for your comfortable retirement; save.

295   Resolve to begin each day with a sense of purpose, and finish with a sense of accomplishment.

296   Resolve to fast, to cleanse your body of toxic impurities, and your mind of toxic thoughts, feelings and behaviors.

297   Resolve never to tell a child that they are not smart or cannot do what they are passionate about.

298   Resolve to hear people out, let them make their point, consider their opinions and point of view in a humble, receptive and thoughtful manner.

299   Resolve to make major changes in small steps.

300   Resolve to tell your mother you love her every chance you get.

301   Resolve to seek guidance and direction from the intelligence pervading all things.

Sow v. (sown or sowed, sowing)

1. To scatter (good thought-seed) throughout the mind, over body, and into your heart for growth; plant.

2. To implant, introduce, or promulgate (into the mind); seek to propagate or extend.

   Example:
   Resolve to sow good thought seeds.

302   Resolve to manifest persistence, determination, and endurance for they alone will overcome a lack of talent, genius, and education.

303   Resolve to be single-minded, to steadfastly and tenaciously drive for the one thing on which you have decided.

304   Resolve to use the force of habit to drive you to your goal.

305   Resolve to correct your mistakes the moment they are realized.

306   Resolve to live without regret and without the feeling of guilt.

307   Resolve at the end of each day to awake with a plan of action.

308   Resolve to speak slowly and deliberately, cultivating an attitude of repose and peace.

309   Resolve to avoid talking about your accomplishments or yourself.

310   Resolve to keep your conversations positive and constructive with yourself and others.

311   Resolve to be a person of action and few words. Don't discuss what you are going to do, or what you plan to do, do it. Let your actions do the talking.

312   Resolve to keep your personal business personal, and your private matters out of the public domain.

"Will Power"

You sleep, yet I am awake poised and ready. Though you have forgotten that I exist, I am. Beseeching and summoning prophets and gods whose ears may hear, they cannot act or change the condition of your state and to the one who can, not even a whisper from you. I reside within and I alone have the power to change your fate. I am the gift given you at birth, the one super power you possess. I am the genie in the bottle, your one magic wish. To know my name is not the same as knowing me, I must be called, summoned to action, I must be used.

Closer to you than your eyelash I reside in the marrow of your bones. Who am I? I am your "**Will**" and when summoned to act I become "Will Power".

Kemit Affirmationary
"We become what we emit through time."

313   Resolve to avoid doing what pleases you today but will bring you embarrassment and shame tomorrow. Do not say sorry, say no, thank you.

314   Resolve to apologize quickly when you know you are in the wrong.

315   Resolve to allow others to live without projecting your expectations upon them.

316   Resolve to express interest in the thoughts and ideas of others.

317   Resolve to be aware of your mood and how it affects your ability to make decisions.

318   Resolve to identify and eliminate distractions in your work and in your life.

319 Resolve to maintain good posture at all times; when sitting or standing, walk with your head up, your spine straight, your shoulders back, and your gaze direct and engaged.

320 Resolve to maintain good oral and physical hygiene.

321 Resolve to create and maintain a clean, clutter and chaos-free home and working environment. Put things in their place where they belong and get rid of those things no longer in use.

322 Resolve to maintain your composure when provoked; remain calm, reposed, and serene in mind and bearing.

323   Resolve to create and maintain consistent routines and set times for your exercise, meditation, prayer, work, self-improvement, family, and rest.

324   Resolve not to share your thoughts or ideas with those who are negative and pessimistic.

325   Resolve to convey the attitude and feeling that every individual lives their life according to their own truth.

326   Resolve to listen to others more than they listen to you; talk less.

327   Resolve to mind your own business and affairs, and keep your comments and opinions to yourself, where they can do no harm.

328   Resolve not to say things in public
        that may cause the
        embarrassment of others.

329   Resolve to avoid conversation
        about others who are absent, for
        they are unable to defend
        themselves.

330   Resolve to abstain from sharing
        your opinion on political or other
        divisive issues when it can be
        avoided.

331   Resolve to intuit the meaning of
        things, events, circumstances and
        moment.

332   Resolve to improve your memory.
        Practice memorizing passages,
        significant events, dates, names,
        and small details. Concentrate.

333   Resolve to convert and transmute your pain into the power of persistence and endurance.

334   Resolve to cultivate a united, loving, supportive, and happy household.

335   Resolve to be self-sufficient, rely upon no one to do for you what you can do for yourself.

336   Resolve to cultivate a resolute, decisive, and steadfast will.

337   Resolve to be enthusiastic.

338   Resolve to conduct yourself with integrity and fairness.

339   Resolve to point out mistakes indirectly.

340   Resolve that you will not take things personal when others are giving you advice.

341   Resolve to exemplify confident, competent, stately manners at all times.

342   Resolve to build a reputation of being persistent and determined.

343   Resolve to be synonymous with execution.

344   Resolve to avoid controversy.

345   Resolve to be knowledgeable of the people, things, and events that shape the financial and political landscape of the world.

346 Resolve not to allow small incidents to become elements of major discord in your relationships.

347 Resolve not to be drawn into arguments about unimportant subjects.

348 Resolve to create multiple streams of income.

349 Resolve to pluck from your garden of words and thoughts any manifestation of hesitancy; act deliberately with everything you do.

350 Resolve to overcome all difficulties in your life.

351 Resolve to be one with the universal good in all things.

352   Resolve to consider the lessons concealed in all of life's circumstances and situations.

353   Resolve to practice self-control at all times.

354   Resolve to contemplate your motives, actions, and their consequences before you speak and act.

355   Resolve to walk with a sense of accomplishment and positive self-expectancy.

356   Resolve to be one with your word, do not distort the truth. Lies and half-truths corrupt the spirit.

357   Resolve to do things which fortify your will; that eternal spark of fire which animates your mind and stirs your soul.

358   Resolve to complete all your plans on the date and time you specify.

359   Resolve not to make promises you do not plan to keep.

360   Resolve to exercise restraint when tempted to use your power and authority over others; be humble.

361   Resolve not to internalize the negative or pessimistic attitude of others, show them the power of optimism.

362   Resolve to be an asset an every situation.

363 Resolve to keep master the skill
of concentration, exercise you
will and your power to decide.

364 Resolve to develop your attention
span, focus.

365 Resolve never to allow your
wishes to be the father of facts.

366 Resolve to be impartial when
presented with one side of an
argument. Promote balance, hear
both side before taking action.

367 Resolve to remain detached and
unemotional when presented
with observations and
conclusions reached by others.

368 Resolve to develop your ability to
discern the difference between
important and unimportant facts.

369   Resolve to qualify statements as either conjecture, opinion, fiction or facts, backed by evidence.

370   Resolve to practice accurate thinking, be precise.

371   Resolve to develop your intuitive faculty.

372   Resolve to be authentic.

373   Resolve to give thanks for the blessing you expect to receive each day, each moment.

374   Resolve to smile when you find yourself disappointed or frustrated with the past, it is gone, extract the lesson and move on.

375   Resolve to create routines which promote a positive, expectant mental attitude every evening, every morning you rise from your bed.

376   Resolve that your actions will speak louder than your words.

377   Resolve not to discuss your ideas, or plans with anyone not working with you to achieve them.

378   Resolve to be enthusiastic about what you are trying to achieve.

379   Resolve not to permit your emotions to be your handicap.

380   Resolve to withdraw from the impulse of greed as a motive for your actions.

381   Resolve to refrain from getting involved with or commenting upon the people, things or events which do not concern you.

382   Resolve to study and learn from the best in your industry.

383   Resolve to observe the habits of those you deem successful, make a study of them and commit to learning the most useful.

384   Resolve to abandon thoughts and ideas which have proven, over time, to be unproductive and useless.

385   Resolve to align yourself with the objective of the business, the goal of your leadership, not individual agendas.

386   Resolve to qualify the triggers that make you angry; take away their power.

387   Resolve not affect or infect others with your sour mood. Improve your outlook, employ your imagination and visualize a different interaction and outcome.

388   Resolve to cultivate endurance.

389   Resolve to avoid trying to impress others.

390   Resolve to live within your means.

391   Resolve to keep, honor and deliver upon your promises.

392   Resolve that you will not pretend to be something you are not, be yourself.

Inspiration

Being in the right environment and having the right people around you when planting and cultivating purposeful thoughts, ideas and dreams, is paramount to your success. Therefore, when planting and sowing good thought seeds, discern the energy of your environment and those around you. Are the conditions conducive to what you are trying to achieve? If the environment, people and energy are not conducive to your needs, wait for a better time to plant.

393   Resolve not to make important decisions when emotional, excited, or under the influence of drugs or duress.

394   Resolve to prepare, to practice until you know without doubt or hesitation that you can do what you have to do.

395   Resolve to reconcile your differences with others; work to identify agreeable points, then agree to reconvene to discuss the matters of disagreement.

396   Resolve to create and foster effective and productive habits.

397   Resolve to refrain from commenting upon or discussing the mistakes or ill-fortunes of others.

398   Resolve not to be dramatic, bring calm to the situation.

399   Resolve not to complain about known problems; rather try to find a solution quietly.

400   Resolve to take action on what you learn.

401   Resolve to acknowledge the faith of others, and never force your faith or beliefs upon them.

402   Resolve to spend no time with self-pity.

403   Resolve not to be led astray from your purpose, though the odds appear to be against you.

404   Resolve to repel any manifestation of complacency.

405   Resolve to break your task, objectives and goals into small manageable steps.

406   Resolve to identify methods and tools for measuring your progress; if it cannot be measured it will not be improved.

407   Resolve to be vigilant about making decisions based upon unfounded or groundless accusations.

408   Resolve to be Lord and Master of your thoughts, actions, deeds and character.

409   Resolve not to be dogmatic.

410   Resolve not to comment, give suggestions or opinions, to others when they are venting their frustrations with people or circumstances; let them vent and don't judge.

411   Resolve to be an asset not a liability to yourself and your family.

412   Resolve to impregnate your intentions, your actions, ideas, plans and your aim with good will and love.

413   Resolve to live life forward, not backwards.

414   Resolve not to rehash or relive hurtful, disappointing, highly charged discussions or incidence.

415 Resolve to repel the inclination to always be right or to prove others wrong.

416 Resolve to make a practice and habit of clear, concise, written and verbal communication.

417 Resolve to evolve, to change, to develop slowly into a better, more complete, more advanced and wiser human being.

418 Resolve to imagine future conversations and possible outcomes.

419 Resolve to visualize your day with more specificity.

420 Resolve to make a habit of forecasting.

421 Resolve to visualize future events.

422 Resolve to thwart the impulse to second guess yourself; make a decision and take action.

423 Resolve to have a bias towards action.

424 Resolve to seek the sensation which accompanies being productive.

425 Resolve to foster a desire for closure; finish what you start.

426 Resolve to be cognizant of your blind spots.

427 Resolve to commit to professional development.

Inspiration

Exercise your power to choose. We exercise our power to choose every day. We exercise our power to choose when we decide to do this or that, when we decide to go or not go. We exercise our power to choose when we decide to do this task before doing that task. We exercise our power to choose when we entertain the idea of productive and unproductive thought. We exercise our power to choose when we fail to make a decision. We exercise our power to choose when we decide to change and also when we decide through indecision to remain the same. We exercise our power to choose when we contemplate the chances for our failure or our success. Exercise your power to choose, make a choice, decide and see your decision through.

428   Resolve to treat children with deference and respect.

429   Resolve to teach your children to be self-sufficient.

430   Resolve to teach your children how to express gratitude.

431   Resolve to practice the art of listening well.

432   Resolve to value the importance of family.

433   Resolve to take nothing for granted.

434   Resolve to accept the fact that anything good requires effort and work.

435   Resolve to do it right the first time.

436   Resolve to be unwilling to take shortcuts.

437   Resolve to minimize risk taking when you're fatigued.

438   Resolve to know when to stop.

439   Resolve to make plans only when you are sober.

440   Resolve to consult with your calendar before making commitments.

441   Resolve to chase all your alcoholic drinks with a glass of water; don't over consume, maintain your composure.

442   Resolve to respect the time of others.

443 Resolve to know when to say when, know and respect your limits and the limits of others.

444 Resolve to know when you are out of sorts and be willing to ask your friends for assistance.

445 Resolve to know when to ask for help.

446 Resolve to know when to take a moment, step back.

447 Resolve to know the signs of illness.

448 Resolve to respect the law and cooperate with peace officers.

449 Resolve to maintain your equipment.

450 Resolve to be observant of your surroundings and environment.

451 Resolve to practice vigilance.

452 Resolve to be curious about other cultures.

453 Resolve to allow time for recovery.

454 Resolve to seek and promote a balanced view.

455 Resolve to respect your body.

456 Resolve to give people the time and the space to process their experience.

457 Resolve to acknowledge the duality within and know which one is resistant to change.

458   Resolve to stick to your routines and adjust them only after much consideration.

459   Resolve to push through the pain, increase your tolerance for growth.

460   Resolve to inconvenience as few people as possible.

461   Resolve to ask God for nothing, but show appreciation for everything.

462   Resolve to give people the benefit of doubt.

463   Resolve to give people the benefit of positive intent.

464   Resolve to know that it is not necessary or warranted to comment upon the observations of others; because you hear does not obligate you to speak.

465   Resolve to gracefully end your discussions with those who refuse to consider others points of view.

466   Resolve to guard against expressing personal opinions or beliefs as if they are certainly correct and cannot be doubted.

467   Resolve not to over commit to your friends, family and work.

468   Resolve to be mindful and respectful when relying upon the time and resources of another.

469 Resolve not to participate in one-upmanship.

470 Resolve to expend no effort to find fault or deficiencies in people or things; change the subject when others are doing so.

471 Resolve to profit from your losses.

472 Resolve to explore.

473 Resolve to be flexible and understanding.

474 Resolve to avoid annoying others with repeated questions, request or complaints.

475 Resolve to look for reasons to laugh.

476 Resolve to excuse yourself when confronted by loud and argumentative people. Stay calm, speak softly and unemotionally and walk away.

477 Resolve to appeal to your family and friends more noble motives.

478 Resolve to examine, identify, leverage and employ your resources.

479 Resolve to repay all debt.

480 Resolve not to be misleading, and know when you are being misled.

481 Resolve to constantly appeal to your own more noble motives.

482 Resolve to excuse yourself if you believe you are likely to lose your composure.

483   Resolve to maintain your professional and personal relationships.

484   Resolve not to waste time on unproductive thoughts and feelings.

485   Resolve to unearth the subconscious ideas that dissuade you from leaving your comfort zone.

486   Resolve to commit to professional development.

487   Resolve to commit to personal development.

488   Resolve to re-create yourself.

489   Resolve to avoid trying to impress people with words; be succinct, always say less than is necessary.

490   Resolve to find time to meditate daily.

491   Resolve to practice the art of listening well.

492   Resolve to take nothing for granted.

493   Resolve to accept the fact that all things worthwhile require effort, work.

494   Resolve to do things right the first time.

495   Resolve to be unwilling to take shortcuts.

496   Resolve to minimize risk taking when you're fatigued.

497   Resolve to know when to stop.

498   Resolve to stretch and do Yoga.

499   Resolve to study and seek to understand how your thoughts manifest themselves in your character and environment.

500   Resolve not to be the source of hearsay or controversy.

501   Resolve to know that most times an explanation for your actions is not required.

502   Resolve to make time to declutter your mind and your environment.

503   Resolve not contribute to discussions about the problems, misfortunes or mistakes of others, unless the discussions involves solutions.

504   Resolve to avoid repeating yourself, and retelling old stories; and don't repeat what others tell you.

505   Resolve to dissuade yourself and others from rehashing or reliving past conflicts and emotionally charged events.

506   Resolve to know that the people who talk about others people to you, are talking about you to other people.

507   Resolve to develop and evolve your situational awareness tree.

508   Resolve to learn how to qualify
and quantify risk.

509   Resolve to decline giving
relationship advice, but rather
help the person to uncover what
it is they need from their
relationships.

510   Resolve not to dwell on the past.

511   Resolve to shut out all thoughts
that weaken, interfere with, or
make timid your resolve.

512   Resolve to perfect your conduct.

513   Resolve to know that others
cannot stop, deter or distract you
from doing what you need to do
unless you permit them to do so;
exert your will.

514   Resolve to blame no one for your failure.

515   Resolve to study and solve your own problems.

516   Resolve to seek out women and men who know more than you and listen to what they have to say.

517   Resolve to keep your attention and your will centered upon what you are trying to achieve.

518   Resolve to control the fleeting impulses of your mind and will.

519   Resolve to practice centering your attention by mastering your will.

520 Resolve to practice forming in your mind a mental image, a picture of what it is you earnestly seek.

521 Resolve to be on the lookout for opportunities to practice self-control.

522 Resolve not to over react to unpleasant news; immediately look for the lesson and opportunity which others will fail to see.

523 Resolve to practice suppressing your desire.

524 Resolve to make time to review your actions during the day, endeavor to uncover your mistakes, missed opportunities, and possible improvements.

525 Resolve to be free of all signs that show a lack of self-control.

526 Resolve to give more than you take; make a habit of contributing.

527 Resolve to declutter your mind and your environment of all that it not useful.

528 Resolve to enter a room quietly, observe the setting, people, mood and conversations; don't be imposing nor should you disrupt the flow, rather enter slowly, mindful of the dynamics.

529 Resolve not to boast about the advice you have given to others; the wise have no reason to brag.

530   Resolve to know that just because one expects something from you, it doesn't mean that you have to fulfill their expectations.

531   Resolve to know that discomfort is an interruption.

532   Resolve to know that for every high there is a low; for every low there is a high.

533   Resolve to be the best you can possibly be.

534   Resolve to replace the word try with, I am going to.

535   Resolve to refrain from using unpleasant memories to make your point.

536   Resolve to acknowledge the fact that what is important to you may not always be important to others.

537   Resolve to resist the compulsion to share your ideas with those who you know have little interest in them.

538   Resolve to remember where you put things.

539   Resolve to avoid commenting upon what is inappropriate and appropriate behavior.

540   Resolve to be sensitive to the needs of your spouse or partner.

541   Resolve to give people there space.

542   Resolve to give people the opportunity to explain themselves.

543   Resolve not to share the personal, private details of your friends and family.

544   Resolve not to ask people probing, personal questions.

545   Resolve to mind your own business.

546   Resolve to spend no time discussing or interpreting the actions of others when they don't involve you.

547   Resolve not to level accusations. If required to speak, state your innocence plainly and without emotion.

548   Resolve not to accuse others
when things go missing.

549   Resolve to be resilient.

550   Resolve to accept the fact that
you cannot please everyone.

551   Resolve to live your values.

552   Resolve to cherish the joy of
giving.

553   Resolve to go high when they go
low.

554   Resolve to be honest about your
feelings.

555   Resolve to keep it moving;
forward.

556   Resolve to let the bad things go.

557   Resolve to create quiet zones and
        quiet times in your home.

558   Resolve to establish ground rules
        and boundaries when sharing
        space with family and friends.

559   Resolve not to allow discord in
        one relationship to cause
        disharmony in other.

560   Resolve never to look down
        upon the destitute, the needy
        or the homeless. Send them
        good vibes, and affirm silently
        that the highest good shall be
        done for them.

You can do it.

How long have you put off taking action on something you believe in because you fear making a mistake, or because you think people will not like your idea?

I know the feeling, we all do.

The fear of making mistakes is worse than making the mistake. So what if you make a mistake? So what if you don't succeed on your first, second, third, fourth or even fifth attempt. If you are unwilling to make mistakes and fail, how can you ever expect to accomplish anything?

Resolve to make as many mistakes as are necessary to reach your goals and objectives.

Inspiration

Our best ideas and dreams evade us primarily because we lack courage and humility. Mostly we fear what others will think and say if we make a mistake. We fear the hypothetical loss more than we cherish the potential gains which are just as possible, and more likely. Without the courage to fail we never try, and lacking humility, we lack the fortitude to make the mistakes which enable us to grow.

Resolve to evolve, you can do it.

Acknowledgement

Humanity at its best, when we help each other to be our best, live to our highest potential and cooperate to do the most good for the most people. It is with this belief that I have committed myself through the years help others create mental and physical environments conducive to their success. To do so I searched diligently for books and individuals from whom I could learn and grow. For this reason I can claim no ownership or authorship for the words within these pages. I humbly thank those cosmic and earthly teachers and mentors who inspired me, who challenged me one day to channel their thoughts, visions, and ideals into a garden which would one day benefit humanity; thank you.

I would like to give special thanks to Possibility Advocates Angela Robinson, Mary and Michael Adair, Eva Janos,

Mark Klopfer and Debbie Shotwell. Thank you for your encouragement and support.

I would also like to thank my lovely wife, Marie-France L'Esperance-Robinson, and my lovely daughter Shamaine L'Esperance Robinson for your continued love, understanding, commitment and support. Thanks for giving me the time and space to complete what I started.

Last but not least, I want to thank my mother, Bertha Mae Robinson. You taught me that "nothing beats a try but a fail"; and to this I would add, "Nothing beats a try but a fail, and failure is sweetest when you have given your all, knowing with certainty, you had no more to give." Give life everything you have, leave nothing on the table.

Share-it-forward

If any of the resolutions within this garden have improved your outlook in any way, share-it-forward with a family member, friend, co-worker, stranger, or someone you believe could benefit from its reading. Together we will re-create our eternal Garden of Eden within the hearts and minds of humanity.

We support local job creation. To purchase additional copies for family, friends, or co-workers, please make a request at your local bookstore or visit us online:
http://www.ResolvedToEvolve.com or
http://www.KemitAffirmationary.com
Coming Spring 2017

About the Author

At early age, Virgil E. Robinson knew he wanted to be an author, but a disparaging comment from a teacher crushed this dream for a time. The experience however taught him to never discourage anyone from pursuing their passion. At the University of San Jose State, Virgil studied Biological and Cognitive Psychology. Passionate about encouraging people, he went on to have a successful career in the Silicon Valley as a retained Executive Coach and Candidate Advocate. In this capacity, his biggest task lay in helping professionals overcome their internal critic.

In 2008, while battling his own internal critic, Virgil coined the phrase "Possibility Advocate", and founded the Possibility Advocate Society (PAS) and the

Possibility Advocate Gear (PAG). PAS provides encouragement, and the PAG provides funding to individuals who need capital to push their dreams forward. Four hundred years from now, Virgil hopes that "Possibility Advocate" will be a permanent part of the human lexicon, and PAG the largest grantor of funds to passionate dreamers all over the world.

Possibility Advocate

Possibility Advocates are impartial servants of humanity, servants of the dreamers. They help family, friends, strangers, and themselves to transcend limitations both internally and externally. Rather than assume the role of the Devil's Advocate, they help to find the reasons why ideas will work and succeed, rather than why they will not.

The next time you or a family member has an idea, take a moment to *dream* with them. If you are a good planner, help them to *plan*. If you are better at executing, help them to take *action*. And if you are better at analysis, help them consider the results of their efforts and encourage them to *repeat* the dream-plan-act process until they finally succeed.

http://www.PossibilityAdvocate.com
Advocate possibility, hope, and encourage bold action always.

Made in the USA
Columbia, SC
26 March 2018